Your Next is NOW!
Taking it all back

DR. JOANNA BIRCHETT

DR. JOANNA BIRCHETT

Your NEXT Is NOW! Taking it all back.

Published in the United States of America by Dr. Joanna Birchett. ©2019 at Gospel 4 U Publishing

www.gospel4unetwork.com

All Rights Reserved. No part of this book may be reproduced or transmitted in any way by any means, electronic, mechanical, photocopy, recording or otherwise, without prior permission of the author except as provided by USA copyright law. Scriptures are taken from the **Holy Bible, The King James Version** unless otherwise marked.

ISBN - 978-0-692-36864-0

Printed in the United States of America

September 2019

DR. JOANNA BIRCHETT

DEDICATION

I dedicate this book to my Lord and Savior Jesus the Christ. I am so thankful for the opportunity to be used by Him in any way He desires.

To every person who is moving from their next to the now, I am writing this to cheer you on, this is for

TABLE OF CONTENTS

DEDICATION

ACKNOWLEDGEMENTS

INTRODUCTION

FOREWORD

1. SIGHT TO SEE …………………………..……15
2. OH TASTE! …………….…………….……..…19
3. WHAT TIME IS IT?……………………….…....21
4. FAITH IT OUT!……………………………..…25
5. REVERENCE……………………………....…29
6. NOW MIRACLES…………………………….31
7. TRUST ME…………………………….............33
8. BITTER TURNS BETTER……………………..35
9. FORGIVE NOW!.......................................39
10. FIGHT……………..…………………………41
11. PEACE BE STILL……………………………45
12. IT IS POSSIBLE…………………………..…49
13. THE COMEBACK……………………….....51
14. THE LORD, OUR SHEPHERD…………………53
15. RECEIVE THE VICTORY……………………59

PRAYER & DECLARATION

ACKNOWLEDGEMENTS

I am so grateful for all the love and support of my family; special thanks to my husband, Apostle Larry, for always being there for me. Thank you for believing in the gifts in me .and allowing the Lord to use you to pull them out.

To all my children, you guys give me hope and I go hard so I can lead by example. I want to encourage you all to make sure that Jesus is your everything. You have it in you too, each one of you and I love you all.

FOREWORD

Have you watched others receive their blessings and breakthroughs only to question God about when your turn would come? Have you listened to countless sermons and received numerous confirmations that your promise is on the way but you still haven't embraced it? Or perhaps, you have prayed and stopped praying because nothing appears or seems to be leaning in your favor?

If you can identify with the previous questions and if you are looking for a blueprint that can move you into better then you, my friend, have made an excellent choice by picking up this little goldmine filled with rich nuggets to get you there. The devil does not want you to achieve Your NEXT and the thought-provoking questions will enlighten and heighten your revelation concerning the spiritual battle you are in. You will also discover that you ultimately win!

Dr. Joanna Birchett challenges the reader of this book to reconsider not only who they are but who they serve. She shares in detail the formula that will aid you in receiving

Your NEXT NOW! You will learn how to change your focus from the natural and tap into the spiritual vision given to you by the Father. You will be reminded of the enemy's tactics and how Satan comes to discourage the heart of God's children and how you are to fight against discouragement as it comes.

In ***Your NEXT is NOW***, you will see firsthand that the weapons of your warfare are not carnal and that you have been equipped by way of the Holy Spirit to stand against the wiles of the devil. The enemy does not want you to embrace your NEXT in God; however, Dr. Birchett explores the Holy Scriptures to remind the reader that their faith in the promises of the Lord is manifested through faith and obedience to what God has promised!

This book will teach its reader how to not only fight but remain in the game! The words written herein will become life as the anointing leaps from the pages into your soul, thus prospering your ability to walk in faith and not by sight. This revelation will stir the heart, mind, and spirit into complete activation, causing boldness in the spirit to embrace and reclaim what belongs to them.

If you have trusted the Lord, I encourage you NEVER to give in or give up on that no matter what it looks like or feels like. I am a firm believer that "the eye is a lie" and this is why we are told to walk by faith and not by sight. You are holding a prophetic gem, so eat and allow your soul to digest what has been prepared for you. Remember, you asked the Lord for a sign and an answer to your situation—well… ***Your NEXT Is NOW*** and it is time to start ***Taking It All Back!***

Manifold Blessings,
Apostle Chantell L. Poole, M.Div.

DR. JOANNA BIRCHETT

INTRODUCTION

In life we will always have ups and downs, but if we keep dwelling on the past we will never propel into the NEXT!

I am on an assignment from the Lord and that is to position you to be in ready mode to receive your now. You are reading this book because I was in service one Sunday and my husband, Apostle Larry, walked over and anointed me and began to pour into my spirit; as he prayed and prophesied, he said these words to me: "The Lord says to tell you, 'Your next is now.'"

Immediately this hit me; the words God used my husband to release brought it home for me and I could hear the Lord saying, "Go Joanna, go tell the world to get rid of fear, get rid of hate and past hurts. There is a people waiting for that one word and now is the time. Now is the moment for their change to come."

This book is designed to help everyone, no matter their age

or gender. I pray that every page will help you to connect with the Father so He can release you into the future.

Your NEXT Is NOW is designed to help you get out of the old and move into the new. The enemy tries to bind our sense of sight, but in this book, I decree and declare that you will receive a fresh wind that will open your eyes and you will see clearly.

As you read this book allow the spirit of the Lord to release Himself in you, I prophesy to your NEXT and I call it forth right now in Jesus' Name. Welcome to the NEW!

~1~
SIGHT TO SEE

*Matthew 13:10 This is why I speak to them in parables: **Though seeing, they do not see**; though hearing, they do not hear or understand.*

In this scripture Jesus spoke in parables to the disciples, I always wondered to myself, *Why would Jesus use parables?*

Well, Jesus used parables as a method of teaching; as we look through the Word we often see Jesus using parables. In Matthew 13:10 Jesus' disciples asked Him why He taught in parables. He replied, "To you it has been given to know the secrets of the kingdom of heaven…" Here Jesus is referring to His disciples, the people who followed Him and learned from Him: these people, his disciples, were the ones who were going to understand the parables. They would understand because they had spiritual sight.

Our sight is a gift, one that we use nearly every waking moment of the day. Naturally we take in so much with our eyes: traffic lights, the dishes on the kitchen counter, the blinking cursor on the computer screen, the leaves changing on the trees outside the office. Try to count everything that has crossed your line of vision in the space of an hour, and it's an impossible task.

Listen, the Bible is clear that we MUST have spiritual sight. How can we understand if we cannot first see it in the spiritual realm? We are in a season of taking back our stuff, but I want to help you, beloved; to get it, we must have the ability to see. My father has an eye disease known as glaucoma, this can be a hard thing to deal with, but he does not allow his disability to stop him, with the help of my sister he is working hard to find a way to correct the problem. Listen, my dad had laser surgery on his eyes years ago but it did not fully correct it, what am I saying? Don't allow what you tried in the past to hinder your future—sounds familiar, right? It brings me back to Saul on the Damascus road, he had an encounter with Jesus and the scales were removed and he got sight. We know the history of this man; he was persecuting all the believers, anyone who followed the man named Jesus the Christ. When he met Jesus, it was a moment of truth, everything changed, even his name was changed from Saul to Paul, and all things became new.

Having spiritual sight is very important. I want to help someone today who has been blinded by the cares of life and sometimes we allow people to cause us to get bitter, unforgiving, hateful, jealous, and envious.

Today, I speak to your spirit and with the power of the HOLY SPIRIT invested in me I CALL FORTH FREEDOM in JESUS' name. I once was blind but now I can see. I have tasted, and I see that the Lord is good!

MY NEXT IS NOW!

You will no longer allow

- Financial Issues
- Deportation Issues
- Court Issues
- Jealousy
- Lack
-
- Addiction
- Low Self-esteem

Whatever you are going through, write it here_____

This will no more have you blinded.

Now, I want you to see the situation as Jesus sees it; begin to speak life to this thing, tell **IT** how big you Father in Heaven is, tell **IT** you have the victory over it. **IT** cannot hold you hostage anymore. Today is a brand-new day and you are taking back your spiritual sight, not tomorrow.... RIGHT NOW!

~2~
OH TASTE!

O taste and see that the LORD is good: blessed is the man that trusteth in him. ~ Psalm 34:1

To taste means to eat; discern; perceive; to evaluate. To taste in its verb form refers to the testing of goods by means of the sense of taste. The Apostle Paul and David both spoke of having "Tasted of the heavenly gift." The sense of taste includes most of the other senses—sight, smell, and touch. And certainly, this is also true in spiritual things.

I have learned that there are basically three different classes of Christians:

- There are those who hear without seeing;
- There are those who both hear and see without tasting;
- There are those in whom all three combines—to whom "Faith" cometh by hearing," in whom faith

grows by seeing, in whom faith is developed and consummated by tasting.

After reading this, which category do you find yourself in? Well, listen here, in this season you will be able to taste and see how mighty God is in your life. I want to talk to the person who is in a tasteless season right now, you might not be able to see clearly, but I speak to every fiber in your being and by the power of the Holy Spirit I command you shall see and taste of the goodness of the Lord, in Jesus' name!

Today, I ask the Lord to open your spiritual eyes so you can magnify the supremacy of His glory through our Lord Jesus Christ, in the power of the Holy Spirit, by treasuring all that God is, loving all whom He loves, praying for all His purposes, meditating on all His word, sustained by all His grace. This is my prayer for you.

~3~
WHAT TIME IS IT?

Matthew 11:12 ~ *From the days of John the Baptist until now, the Kingdom of Heaven suffereth violence and they that are violent must take it back by force.*

I can hear a sound in the atmosphere, it's time to take it back, not just take it back but take it ALL BACK!

I am speaking to a people who have lost some stuff, some people who are SICK and tired of the enemy running rampant in their lives.

In order to take anything back, we have to be able to identify the enemy. You must use your spiritual senses to recognize and identify his tricks and devices. It's time for the activation to begin.

– Identify the enemy

The Bible says in **Ephesians 6:12** ~ *For we wrestle not against flesh and blood, but against principalities, against* *powers, against the rulers of the darkness of this world, against spiritual wickedness in high places.*

People are not your problem!

We are fighting incorrectly

That is why we are losing…

People are only a tool used against you.

The TRUE enemy that you are fighting with is a spirit. Not the Holy Spirit but an evil spirit, a messenger of Satan, sent to attack and destroy your hope, joy, peace, your home, your finances, your health and bring CHAOS!

John 10:10A states the thief comes to steal, kill and DESTROY! But I hear the Lord saying EVERYTHING that the Locust, The Palmerworm, the Cankerworms have stolen, get ready to retrieve it all!

– Recognize the enemy:

- ELEVATE YOUR FAITH
- PUT ON THE WHOLE ARMOR
- GET IN POSITION
- STAND YOUR GROUND

- **WATCH GOD MOVE**

> "Just as the Holy Spirit needs a body, evil spirits need one, too, and if you allow them to, they take up residence quickly."
>
> Dr. J

Obedience is doing what God says, when He says it, how He says it, for whatever reason He says it. There's no room for passivity when it comes to obeying the Father. This level of commitment requires an active choice. What will you choose today?

Just as the Holy Spirit needs a body, evil spirits need one, too, and if you allow them to, they take up residence quickly. The devil will not wait for you to change your minds, he has come to steal, kill and destroy and we must always be armed and ready.

I propose to you, sir/ma'am, that it is your time to take it all back. NO MATTER WHAT AND WHO IS COMING AGAINST YOU. This is your season; this is your moment to take back all that belongs to you. "Don't worry about tomorrow," says the Lord, "take it back today."

I feel a fresh wind falling on you right now, I dare you begin to use the power within to call back your stuff, call back your wayward children, call back your marriage, your peace, your finances—come on, RIGHT NOW! Call it ALL back, in Jesus' Mighty Name.

~4~
FAITH IT OUT

For we walk by faith, not by sight: - **2 Cor.5:7**

During the process of working on this book, I was challenged in many areas of my life, God started to remove people, places and things away from me. In the moment of everything happening, I could not understand what was going on. I used to be the type of person who would shut down and shut people out, but when the teacher is giving a test, it is a time to shut up, sit down and learn.

The test was hard and to be very honest I was ready to throw in the towel, but "no pain no prize". My flesh was trying so hard to overpower my spirit, but just like a father He spoke this into my Spirit: "Face IT and by FAITH you will beat IT." This reminded me of the scripture in 2 Corinthians 5:7: We walk by FAITH, it is faith that allows us to face all our fears and it is faith that will take us into the NEXT.

Too many times we run away and we delay the next move of God. Think about this, Jesus could have stayed in the upper room. He could have hidden somewhere. He could have tried to escape. But instead he went straight to Gethsemane and not just for a quiet place to pray. He went there because He knew He would be easily found by those who wanted to kill Him.

> THE TEST WAS HARD AND TO BE VERY HONEST I WAS READY TO THROW IN THE TOWEL, BUT "NO PAIN NO PRIZE". MY FLESH WAS TRYING SO HARD TO OVERPOWER MY SPIRIT, BUT JUST LIKE A FATHER HE SPOKE THIS INTO MY SPIRIT: "FACE IT AND BY FAITH YOU WILL BEAT IT."
>
> Dr. J

It's impossible for any of us to even begin to imagine the weight that was on Jesus' shoulders. He knew what He must do. And even though He implored God in all earnestness for deliverance from the pain, pressure, trial and persecution He completely yielded his own personal will to God's divine plan.

I want to encourage you, no matter what you are facing right now, run toward the challenge; don't allow it to run you. Someone is reading this at this very moment and there is sickness in your body, but I want you to open up your mouth RIGHT NOW and prophesy over your life, **"IT came to you BUT IT does not belong to you."** You are not going down just like that.

You are equipped to win and if Jesus had given up when He was being tortured, when the pain was excruciating, where would we be right now? After Jesus' death there was a resurrection.

When you are a child of God, you do not operate in anything but Faith, it can move mountains. Faith will take you places that money cannot buy and fear will detour your Future. There is a cliché, "Fake it until you make it," but today I propose to you, yes you! Face it and Faith it out. The Bible recalls, in the book of Mark 5:24–34, there was a woman with an issue of blood, she exhausted all her livelihood trying to get help for her bleeding, but it was not until she got to a place of nothing that she realized that she had no other choice but to FAITH IT OUT, she realized that she had to reach Jesus, the author and finisher of her Faith. He had the remedy for her disease, but it would take FAITH to receive it.

I say all this to help you to understand that what was dead still has the power to live. Maybe you are emotionally drained, maybe you are drowning in debt—FACE IT, identify the IT that is holding you hostage. Step out from the crowd and get ready to receive, Jesus of Nazareth is passing by.

Listen, challenge the truth, **FACE IT** and **FAITH IT OUT,** the **NEXT** season of your life begins right **NOW**.

~5~
REVERENCE

Hebrews 12:29
For our God is a consuming fire.

I want to touch on a subject that is truly missing in the body today and that is REVERENCE. Reverence for God is a quality that is missing in much of what masquerades as Christianity today. Instead of the kind of reverence we see demonstrated throughout the Bible, in current times Christianity has adopted a "Jesus-is-my-buddy" attitude that grossly downplays the holiness, power, and righteous wrath of the Sovereign God.

Reverence does not refer to God as what we think he is like, "The Big Guy in the Sky" or "The Man Upstairs." Once we truly know who God is, we reverence Him in our hearts. Even the thief on the cross, after he realized who Jesus was, rebuked the other thief for his irreverence: "Don't you fear God?" he said to the other thief; then he turned to Jesus and honored Him as the King (Luke 23:40–42).

Our God is a consuming fire, He burns away anything that is not like Him and He sets things in order. A Lack of Reverence for Him can cause lack of God's presence, and we understand that without His presence our next is delayed, the next will be waiting on us to get in line.

God is not a man that He should lie, and He desires the very best for us. God is Sovereign and because of that He deserves our BEST, our best praise, our best Worship, our respect and honor. Listen, beloved, I have two words for you. YOUR NEXT!

But your next depends on your reverence for God. If I was you, right where you are at, I would give God a shout because as you are reading this the angels are moving on your behalf. I don't know about you, but I feel a shift in your attitude, shift in your praise, shift in your relationship. If you felt it and gave Him praise you just praised your way into a miracle.

The scripture says He inhabits the praises of His people. Today I want you to stay in His presence and return to a place of reverence for the Lord.

~6~
NOW MIRACLES

John 2:5–8

⁵ His mother saith unto the servants, Whatsoever he saith unto you, do it.

⁶ And there were set there six waterpots of stone, after the manner of the purifying of the Jews, containing two or three firkins apiece.

⁷ Jesus saith unto them, Fill the waterpots with water. And they filled them up to the brim.

⁸ And he saith unto them, Draw out now, and bear unto the governor of the feast. And they bare it.

The Bible talks about many miracles, but today I want to talk to you about the miracle at the wedding in Cana. Jesus went to a wedding with His disciples and His Mother Mary. Now, at the wedding they ran out of wine, Mary turned to Jesus telling Him they ran out, but Jesus responded, "My time is not come yet." Mary turned to the men at the wedding and told them, "Whatever He says, just do it." The men did exactly what Jesus told them and a great miracle happened. The water that filled up in the water pots all turned into wine.

Now, what I want you to see is that this miracle took place on the third day and happened instantly. What am I saying to you? God is getting ready to release a miracle RIGHT NOW! This next wave, this next touch is getting ready to blow your sanctified minds and all it needs to activate it is your now obedience.

Mary believed in her heart, she spoke it out and it happened   The Lord is saying to you that in the next three days a miracle will take place in your life; your sick child is getting ready to be healed, every lack in your life is pronounced dead in Jesus' mighty name. I pronounce a benediction on fear, doubt, low self-esteem and no weapon that is formed against your minds will prosper according to Isaiah 61, in Jesus' name. In this next season, in order to receive the promises of God, the miracles of God, you have to look past people and focus on God. Hey you, get your five loaves and two fishes and get ready for a miracle now.

~7~
TRUST ME

Romans 10:17 ESV- *So faith comes from hearing, and hearing through the word of Christ.*

The sense of hearing is a very important area of our lives as Christians. If for any reason you lose your sight, it does not eliminate you from being connected to God. If we can hear God we can follow His instructions. The Bible says that my sheep HEARS my voice and a stranger they will not follow. If you are reading this and you are not in the will of God, if you are not saved, if you cannot hear His voice this chapter is for you. It is not in God's will that any of us should perish and I want to take this time to help you to build a relationship with the man named Jesus.

In order to trust and believe God we need faith. Faith is the substance of things hoped for and the evidence of things not seen as stated in Hebrews 11:1. The scripture in Romans 10 verse 17 lets us know that faith is gained by hearing the word of God. Now, I challenge you right now to dare yourself to gain more knowledge of God by first giving your life to Him then finding a Bible-teaching ministry and starting to read the Word for yourself.

If you are ready I want you to say this quick prayer after me:

> *Dear God, I know that I am a sinner and there is nothing that I can do to save myself. I confess all my faults to you and you only, please forgive me of all my iniquities and wash me white as snow. I renounce Satan and I pick up the cross and follow you. At this moment I trust Christ alone as the one who bore all my sins when He died on the cross. I believe that Jesus died and is resurrected and is seated on the right hand of the Father and I will see him again in heaven, please write my name in the Lamb's book of life.*
>
> *Thank you for the assurance that you will walk with me through the deep valley. Thank you for hearing this prayer. In Jesus' Name. Amen.*

Glory to God! If you said that prayer by Faith and trust in Jesus Christ, your Next is NOW. Let me be the first to welcome you into your NEXT season of your life. Now, you need to find a Church so you can grow in the Lord. To God be all the Glory!

~8~
BITTER TURNS BETTER

Ephesians 4:31–32, "*Get rid of all bitterness, rage, anger, harsh words, and slander, as well as all types of malicious behavior. Instead, be kind to each other, tenderhearted, forgiving one another, just as God through Christ Jesus has forgiven you.*"

In the book of Ruth we see a series of stories and setbacks. In chapter one Naomi and her husband and two sons left their homeland in Judah on account of famine. Then Naomi's husband died. Her sons married Moabite women and for ten years the women proved to be barren; then her sons died leaving two widows in the house of Naomi. Even though Ruth cleaved to Naomi, chapter one ends with Naomi's bitter complaint: "I went away full and the Lord has brought me back empty. The Almighty has dealt very bitterly with me." I share this story because we can cause things to happen in our lives because we did not seek God first or we seek Him but are not patient enough to wait on His response and we can cause havoc in our lives, this sometimes pushes us into a place named "Bitter".

Naomi changed her name to represent how she felt, but despite of the name change, Ruth was unmoved. I believe that Ruth was in a season called "Next."

She had made up in her mind that Moab was no longer for her and the only way for her to make it to her next was to look past the bitterness, the pain, the loss, and the hurt and focus on Naomi's God.

So many of us desire more, we desire our season to shift, but how do we expect more when we give less? Why would you expect a blessing when you are never a blessing to anyone? What am I saying to you?

God cannot open the access for you until you open your heart to Him; Ruth gave her all and in return she received more. She did not allow her situation to detour her, but instead she was very motivated. People of God, it is time to get "US" in order, if no One believes in you, always believe in yourself. You can do it, the time is now Esther, you are placed right where you are at for such a time as this, be the example, be the change, assume your position and get ready to win.

Ruth is an example of how God can change a life and take it in a direction He has foreordained. We see Him working out His perfect plan in Ruth's life, just as He does with all His children (Romans 8:28). Although Ruth came from a pagan background in Moab, once she met the God of Israel, she became a living testimonial to Him by faith and her next season was now.

DR. JOANNA BIRCHETT

~9~
FORGIVE NOW!

Forgiveness is a deep thing, in order to move into your next, you must release and let go. We are destined to win, but we are also bound to go through, hurt, pain, rejection and more. I am reminded of Joseph, in the Bible that had a dream and he told it to his brothers, and they despised him. They conspired together and put him in a pit and left him for dead, but as we say in Jamaica, "Wah nuh dead, nuh call it duppy" (Jamaican Patios) which means, **(As long as there is life, there is hope)** Never give up.

I am here to tell you that the dream will not die, but you must forgive right away, l believe that Joseph forgave his brothers while he was in the pit, he still loved them, even from the pit, not saying that for a moment he was not angered but he did not allow it to hinder his destiny. The Bible says in 1 Corinthians 13:4A "Love is patient", I thought hard about this and I began to realize that in order for anyone forgive, they have to exhibit the fruit of patience, and to have patience they have to endure some hard troubles, because perseverance produces patience, so they have to go through to enter into their next. You and I are here today because we are enduring, we are not easily shaken nor will we allow the traps and darts to **detour, delay or deny** us. We are overcomers and we will make it, oh yes! we will.

Today I encourage you my brothers and sisters, to move forward by embracing forgiveness, when we do this will also embrace peace, hope, love and joy. Consider how forgiveness can lead you down the path of physical, emotional and spiritual well-being. **Forgive NOW!**

~10~
FIGHT

"No weapon formed against you shall prosper, and every tongue which rises against you in judgment you shall condemn. This is the heritage of the servants of the Lord, and their righteousness is from me." **Isaiah 54:17**

The good thing about this is: Victory is as won—as you are you. The one against us cannot effectively come against the cross. Jesus is, forever and always, high and lifted up. There is no undoing His reign. His opportunities, insights and wisdom are already ours.

Now, if you believe this why are you giving up? Why are you passive? Why the pity parties? Pick up your weapon (THE WORD) and FIGHT! Fight for your marriage, Fight for your children, Fight for your health. FIGHT!

The enemy's only strategy is to make us believe he can undo what Jesus did. The devil is a liar. His only opportunity is a

FAKE and we have FAITH. Listen, no matter how small the faith is, use what you got. The enemy's tricks are old, he tries to divert us left and if we move with him, and take our eyes off the truth, we lose God. But if we stand firm and don't give into his fake, we shall make it to the end and we will move towards the goal of Christ Jesus.

So, let us stand firm in truth, trust in the Lord and lean not to our own understanding. Let us allow it to sink into our mind then into our heart and then down to our feet so that we walk out with such assurance, nothing—no way, no how—can shake us.

The Word is our arsenal, our power and our stand and according to Psalm 28:7 ~ *The Lord is my strength and my shield; my heart trusts in him, and he helps me. My heart leaps for joy, and with my song I praise him.*

Beloved, you are built to last. I want to encourage you, maybe you find yourself in a bad place in your life or maybe you are just feeling as though you are drowning

God is just, but it is His character that defines what being just really is. He does not conform to some outside criteria. Being just brings moral equity to everyone. When there are evil acts, justice demands there be a penalty. Since God is perfect and has never done evil, no penalty would ever be necessary; however, because of His love, God paid the penalty for our evil deeds by going to the cross Himself. His justice needed to be satisfied, but He took care of it for all who will believe in Him.

DR. JOANNA BIRCHETT

~11~

PEACE BE STILL

Mark 4:37–39 King James Version (KJV)

37 And there arose a great storm of wind, and the waves beat into the ship, so that it was now full.

38 And he was in the hinder part of the ship, asleep on a pillow: and they awake him, and say unto him, Master, carest thou not that we perish?

39 And he arose, and rebuked the wind, and said unto the sea, Peace, be still. And the wind ceased, and there was a great calm.

As I was reading these passages of scripture, I asked the Lord what He wanted me to say in this chapter.

And he said, "PEACE, BE STILL!"

I want you to feel it in the depth of your soul.

Say this with everything in you right now…

The Bible says that there arose a great storm, I want you to stay right there with me. A storm was getting ready to hit them, but Jesus was on the boat and the disciples began to panic. "Lord, don't you care? Master, do you not even care that we are going to die?"

"Lord, do you not see that my bills are overdue?"

"Lord, do you not see that the sickness is getting worse?"

We have all asked one of these questions.

See when things are going great, we never question God's compassion. But God's compassion is not measured by our circumstances nor is His kindness limited to our understanding. God cares just as much when the storm is raging as when the seas are calm and the sun is shining. His mercy is not limited to the sunlight or to the stillness of the waves.

When I read this, it hit me all over again, "and there arose a great storm," the wind began to pick up and the waves rocked the boat. But watch this, as I read further, the Bible said that Jesus got up and rebuked the storm and spoke to the sea "Peace… Be still."

"And the wind ceased," just like that! Did you get that?

Well, if you didn't. Listen! There was a storm but in the midst of any storm there is PEACE, you have to activate it with your voice added with faith. The Bible says that at that very moment, the wind died down, just like that. The very storms in our lives will cease and desist suddenly … when we open our faith-filled mouths!

The literal translation of "be still," taken from the Greek, is—hush! And in modern terms: shut up! And in my Jamaican term, cease and settle.

However you decide to say it, open up your mouth and speak to that storm, your next is voice activated and the sound must be released in order for the earth to move and bring manifestation. The Bible is very straight and in Psalm 103:20 it states, *Bless the Lord, you His angels, who excel in strength, who do His word, heeding the voice of His word.*

Notice that the verse says that angels are "heeding the **voice** of His word." Now, who gives voice to God's Word? We do! Each time we speak God's Word, we give voice to His Word. And when angels hear His Word given voice, they respond!

The Bible says that at the end of Daniel's three weeks of fasting and praying for an answer from God, the angel

Gabriel appeared to him and said to him, "I have come because of your words" (Daniel 10:12).

So, when angels hear you saying, "Thank You, Father, no evil shall befall me nor shall any plague come near my dwelling," (see Psalm 91:10), they will come to your aid because you are giving voice to God's Word. Even if you cannot quote the verse perfectly, they can still come to your rescue.

Now, I say all this to help you understand that even though you see the storm, if you speak God's words it activates the angels to move, so right now I say PEACE, BE STILL and as the angels move watch your season change into the NEXT.

.

~12~
IT IS POSSIBLE

Jesus looked at them and said, "With man this is impossible, but with God all things are possible."
(Matthew 19:26, NIV)

Are you facing something today that seems impossible? With man it may be, but with God ALL things are possible. If you seem to be in an impossible situation, get "with God!" Sometimes it's so easy to focus on our problems and try to solve them in our own strength. But remember, the battle belongs to the Lord. He has a plan for your victory. He has a plan to give you a way out. He is making the things that seem impossible possible. You can trust Him today.

The Bible says that He has plans for your good, not for evil, to give you a future and a hope. Start believing and confessing today, "I am with God, and with God all things are possible!" Are your bills piling up? With God all things are possible. Do your relationships need healing? With God all things are possible. Is there sickness in your body? With God all things are possible! As you meditate on God's Word, His power is activated in your life. He will strengthen you and lead you forward into that place of victory He has in store for you.

~13~
THE COMEBACK

So he that goeth in to his neighbour's wife; whosoever toucheth her shall not be innocent. Men do not despise a thief, if he steal to satisfy his soul when he is hungry; But if he be found, he shall restore sevenfold; he shall give all the substance of his house (**Prov 6:29–31 KJV**).

My purpose is to challenge you the reader to realize that the time is now, we are in a season of TAKING IT ALL BACK!

I came to prophesy to someone right now, you've been overlooked, left out, passed over, talked about, but your next is NOW!

Every dream that you desire is about to find you, I'm talking to someone today who has watched other people get blessed, get healed, get promoted, get their deliverance. And it looks to you from all-natural evidence that it will never be you.

But the Lord said to tell you it's here, do not become weary in well doing for in due season you shall reap if you faint not.

The Lord said to tell you to take the limits off Him, don't allow what you see to detour you. The setback was for the comeback. Beloved, He is doing a new thing right now in you.

I am so excited for you, this is your moment, this is your time. Man of God/Woman of God, this is it. Everything that was stolen is coming right back at you. This is THE COMEBACK!

~14~
THE LORD, OUR SHEPHERD

Psalm 23:1

The Lord is my shepherd, I shall not want

In the book of Psalms chapter 23 a very familiar chapter,

A chapter that is very comforting and sobering

When you read the Scriptures you begin to realize that we are actually reading your past, what are you saying Dr. J?

I KNOW, I just lost a few of you BUT the Scriptures was not written TODAY they were written way back when…. So when we Read, Receive and Release the word, we are PROPHETICALLY DECLARING it in our ATMOSPHERE and OUR LIVES, Not because of us but because IT IS ALREADY DONE! God's word RESUSCITATES us back to life

The devil will try to PERVERT the Word of God but my brothers and sisters when you STAND on God's WORD. You will not fail

In Psalm 23 we all recite this when we are in a bad situation, when we feel afraid or just because. Whatever the reason we read or say this, we are proclaiming as verse 1 tells us that THE LORD IS OUR SHEPHERD. You have to Know who you are and whose you are, we will not take anything back unless we understand this and when you don't know who you are, it make it easy for the enemy, he will come at you and seduce you easily, like Eve or tell you what the flesh desires. But wait a minute!

When the enemy speaks we have to use authority we have and let him know that, who he is dealing with, Use your Authority, back him up and speak the Word of God over your mind, body and Spirit, let him know that, you know too much about HIM and he cannot let you doubt him, because THE LORD IS MY SHEPHERD! And because he is the Lord YOUR Shepherd. He protects you, he covers you.

Listen! The Shepherd stays close to the sheep, this reveals the close relationship that HE has with US. In this Psalm David uses the imagery of God as a shepherd to paint a picture of how LOVING, how CARING and how

PROTECTIVE God is of us

With God as our shepherd, there is no good thing that he would withhold from them that love him.

AND because of that He makes US lie down in green pastures.

What is Green pastures? He gives us PLENTY, He SUSTAINS US!!! HIS Word is GREEN PASTURE. And it is all THAT we need.

The BIBLE says He leads me beside the STILL waters. He gives me peace.

HE RESTORES MY SOUL

Every now and again just like a sheep, we stray, we mess up, we are ready to throw in the towel. BUT HE RESTORES OUR SOUL. He will be there with arms wide open. Just like the PRODIGAL SON. He is waiting to FORGIVE us and RESTORE us again… And again, and again. Come on, you better shout right there. THIS IS A PROMISE!

He leads me in paths of righteousness for his name's sake.

The Lord promises to lead us in paths of righteousness, AND HIS PROMISES ARE YES AD AMEN!! So, we do not have to worry or fear because HE leads us for HIS name sake, HIS PURPOSE, HIS name is full of power and assurance. Even though I walk through the valley of the shadow of death, I will fear no evil, for you are with me; here David acknowledges the reality that life sometimes takes us to dark and desolate places.

LISTEN! This is the key VERSE RIGHT HERE……

We find that yes… He is

- EL SHADDAI – God ALMIGHTY
- El ROI – The God who sees me
- ALPHA AND OMEGA – The beginning and the end

But WE will go through valley experiences, experiences that seem dry, dead, desolate. BUT it is only a shadow, Because THE LORD IS OUR SHEPHERD!

The Bible declares in the book of **Deuteronomy 31:6 ESV**

Be strong and courageous. Do not fear or be in dread of them, for it is the Lord your God who goes with you. He will not leave you or forsake you.

Hebrews 13:5 ESV *~ Keep your life free from love of money, and be content with what you have, for he has said,*

"I will never leave you nor forsake you."

The Lord walks with us through seasons of darkness and despair. Even in the bleakest, blackest times of life, we don't have to fear ANYTHING because our God is with us.

The enemy uses what we see to determine where we will be.

But it is only a shadow. It cannot take you out. THE LORD YOUR SHEPHERD

IS A WAYMAKER

A DELIVERER

A PROMISE KEEPER

A ROCK IN A WEARY LAND

A KEEPER

HE IS THE LORD OUR SHEPHERD!!!

And Just like he did for DAVID..

Today I came to Prophesy to you, yes you!

Do not be moved at what you see, or what you might be going through. Surely GOODNESS and MERCIES are yours FOREVER!! Not just for this Moment. It is NEVER ending. REMEMBER THIS!

The Lord is your Shepherd, He watches, He protects, He sustains, He our keeper and we shall not lack.

~15~
RECEIVE THE VICTORY

"But thanks be to God, who always leads us as captives in Christ's triumphal procession and uses us to spread the aroma of the knowledge of him everywhere **(2 Corinthians 2:14, NIV)**

Have you ever noticed that you often face your greatest attacks when you're about to give birth to the promises of God? Your dreams are placed in your heart by the Lord, but the enemy will try any tactics that he can to try to **disrupt, delay** or even **detour** you. The enemy waits until you're close to the **promotion,** close to the **promise**, ready for the **prize** or when you are fulfilling God's **purpose.** He'll strike when you're just about to step up to a new level. Don't be surprised if you face opposition or go through a disappointment.

That simply means you're about to give birth to what God has placed in your heart. The good news is the forces that are for you are greater than the forces that are against you. Your destiny cannot be stopped by a bad break, by disappointments, by opposition or by other people. God always causes you to triumph. He says, "No weapon formed against you will ever prosper."

We must walk in that, believe that, fight for the victory by putting on the whole armor of God and not allowing Defeat to be an option. My brothers and sisters, you were created to soar, you are destiny believers and we have the victory, so with that I ask you this, are you ready to move into your now? If you said yes, GET UP, shake yourself loose and take it NOW, it is your time!

PRAYERS & DECLARATIONS

PRAYER OF RELEASE

Father, in the name of Jesus, thank you for loving us. I pray that every reader receives all that you have for them to gain from this book; I pray that they are fed by your words and their hearts have opened up with expectancy ready to move into their NOW season. Spirit of the living God cause them to feel a difference after each chapter and release them from every bondage and shame.

Thank you in advance for blessing us and always causing us to triumph.

In Jesus' mighty name… AMEN

DECLARATION

Lord I thank you in advance that my future cannot look like my past because it has already been done in Jesus mighty name.

I am walking away from what was and walking into what is.

I am already a winner

I am prophetically declaring that I am living in my NEXT season.

I am living in the season that God has designed intentionally for me to be in.

Now I am shouting from the mountain top, right here, right now.

Devil, YOU LOST!

PRAYER TO BREAK CYCLES

Father in the name of Jesus, I come against ANY dart that has been sent and by the power of the Holy Spirit I return to sender EVERYTHING meant to harm me and my family in Jesus Name.

I break every cycle, every generational curse, every negative words, everything that is not like you off my life, off my finances, off my children, the BLOOD of Jesus breaks EVERY CYCLE, RIGHT NOW! In Jesus mighty name.

IT IS SO..

AND SO IT IS!

DECLARATION

I Decree and Declare that the Favor of God finds you today

I Decree and Declare that according to Psalm 23:1, you will recognize the Lord as YOUR Shepherd.

I Decree and Declare that you shall Not have NO MORE LACK

I Decree and Declare that every cycle that had you bound is LOOSE right now by the power of the Holy Spirit

I Decree and Declare that just as the 3 Hebrew boys were in the fire, but they came out and did not smell like smoke!!

You shall COME OUT UNTOUCHED, in Jesus mighty name.

Thank You

Blessings Beloved,

I am praying for you, and I know you are destined for great things, Thank you for your purchase of this book and understand this, if the enemy could take you out he would have done so a long time ago, so stand your ground and do not give him any access in your life.

You are stronger than you think, and your destiny is in God's hands. I prophetically declare the blessings of God that makes one rich and adds NO sorrow to it over YOU right now. I pray that you were blessed by this book and I thank God in advance for your victories.

Lastly, the Lord sent me to tell you, YOUR NEXT IS NOW!

Walk in it.

> Prophetess Dr. Joanna Birchett
>
> Co-Pastor – Harvest House Restoration Center
>
> CEO/Founder – Gospel 4 U Network

DR. JOANNA BIRCHETT

ABOUT THE AUTHOR

Dr. Joanna Birchett is a woman on a mission, she has a passion for women and she will not allow anything to stand in the way of what God has called her to do.

Dr Birchett was born in Jamaica and now currently resides in Carlisle, Pennsylvania. Her motto is "Defeat is NOT an Option" and she has dedicated her life to living this thing out. Dr. Birchett holds two Master's degrees, one in pastoral counseling and the other is her Master of Education and she is the proud recipient of an honorary doctorate degree in humanitarian.

Dr. Birchett co-pastors with her wonderful husband Apostle Larry Birchett, Jr. in Carlisle, Pennsylvania at their Church Harvest House Restoration Center.

To request Dr. Birchett for engagements, please contact her via email at Joanna.birchett@gmail.com or call 754-444-8688

www.ingramcontent.com/pod-product-compliance
Lightning Source LLC
Chambersburg PA
CBHW042333150426
43194CB00001B/39